Khushwant Singh, is one of India's most respected authors, a widely syndicated columnist and a journalist with an unenviable reputation of 'holding a mirror to our face... of being frank but not venomous, fearless but not intimidating'. In the recent years his ability to make Indians laugh at themselves, at their own foibles, has earned him the sobriquet of the "greatest humourist of modern India".

Born in 1915, in Hadali, Punjab, Khushwant Singh was educated at Government College, Lahore, and at King's College and the Inner Temple in London. After a brief law practice at Lahore High Court and a stint with the Ministry of External Affairs, he shot to literary fame with his award-winning novel *Train to Pakistan* and the two-volumed *History of the Sikhs*. His other works include *Delhi, The Company of Women* and *India: An Introduction*. He distinguished himself as editor of *The Illustrated Weekly of India* (1969-1979), and *The Hindustan Times* (1980-1983).

He lives in Delhi and devotes his time to writing and other literary activities.

Khushwant Singh's

Joke Book 6

Orient Paperbacks

DELHI | MUMBAI | HYDERABAD

www.orientpaperbacks.com

ISBN : 978-81-222-0314-1

1st Published 2002
16th Printing 2011

Khushwant Singh's Joke Book 6

© Mala Dayal

Illustrated by Arul Raj
Cover design by Vision Studio

Published by
Orient Paperbacks
(A division of Vision Books Pvt. Ltd.)
5A/8 Ansari Road, New Delhi-110 002

Printed in India at
Saurabh Printers Pvt. Ltd., Noida

Cover Printed at
Ravindra Printing Press, Delhi-110 006

INTRODUCTION

The biggest Joke of recent years is that in a nation as humourless as us Indians, joke books sell like hot *Pakoras*. This is the sixth compilation of jokes culled from my columns in *The Hindustan Times* and *The Tribune* to be published by Orient Paperbacks. Every one of the earlier books in the series has gone into more than a dozen reprints. They are to be seen on pavement, railway station and airport book stalls as well as book stores extending from Murree (Pakistan) to Chittagong (Bangladesh). Not many people know me as a novelist, writer of short stories, a historian of the Sikhs or translator from Urdu to English but as a compiler of Jokes. No one takes me seriously; I am a joker. Wherever I happen to be, men and women cluster round me and demand, '*Koi Joke-Shoke ho jai*'— tell us the latest joke.

My latest discovery is that my fellow countrymen are about the most laughable in the world today. Nowhere else will you find so much disparity between what they say and what they mean. We proclaim that we are a spiritual people indifferent to material well-being; in fact, we are more obsessed with many than most others. We have reduced our religions into a meaningless rituals with a lot of mumbo-jumbo of prayers in languages we do not understand. That provides good material for a satirist. Our politicians are even better material than purveyors of spiritualism. They are constipated with self-esteem and let off a lot of malodorous gas all the time. Ask them what they do for a living and nine out of ten will answer 'social service' or *'desh-kee-sewa'*—serving the country. As a matter of fact it is self-service, *'peyt pooja'* (worship of their own bellies) and *'kissa kursee ka'* —stick to seats of importance. Writing angrily about them serves no purpose as they are accustomed to using abusive language against each other. The most effective weapon to puncture their inflated egos is to make fun of them and make them appear as ridiculous as they are.

Getting people to laugh is not easy. Laughter should be spontaneous not artificial. The funniest things I have come across lately are Laughter Clubs. Men and women assemble in parks or beaches and at a given signal break into guffaws of laughter when there is nothing to laugh about. They sound like male and female donkeys braying in unison. Having gone through the exercise with smiles of smug satisfaction on their faces they return to their homes. They have finished with their quota of laughter for the next twenty-four hours.

We Indians do not really have a tradition of humour. Examples cited by Lee Seigel in his *Laughing Matters* comprise restricted repertory of humourous anecdotes. Most of them are about men in high positions being cuckolded by their wives or holy men impregnating their women admirers. Episodes attributed to Raja Birbal and Mulla Do Piaza, Tenali Raman and Gopal Bhore are likewise too crass to pass the test of sophisticated humour. The bulk of our so-called humour is largely ethnic; one community finding traits in another laughable, mothers-in-law versus daughters-in-law and that kind of low-brow jesting. You have to tickle your armpits to get out giggle.

Indian humourists learnt sophistication from the West, largely England and the United States. Since there is no copyright on jokes, they lifted western jokes, changed western name like Tom, Dick and Harry into Santa, Banta and Ghanta to make them appear Indian. I have to sift through this kind of brazen-faced plagiarism week after week to find something genuinely Indian. It is no easy task, I assure you.

Do I make any jokes myself? I am not sure. But I have been in situations which other people find comic and laugh uproariously when I narrate them. I am prone to blurting out what comes to my mind in situations which do not warrant witticism. And as a result get into deep trouble. One I recall happened in London when I was

Press attache to the Indian High Commissioner V.K. Krishna Menon, a singularly humourless character. One day the evening papers carried an announcement of the death of Rani of Mandi, a celebrated beauty of her times. Photographs of her younger days appeared at the front page. Next day in my office arrived a tall Englishman dressed in black carrying a parcel in his hand. He introduced himself: 'I am Kenyon of Kenyon & Kenyon Undertakers. No doubt you have heard of us!"

I replied: 'Indeed I have.' Their funeral parlours with ornate coffins in the windows could be seen all over London.

'No doubt you read of the death of Her Highness the Rani of Mandi!'

I admitted I had read about it in the previous day's evening papers.

'Wasn't I sad?' asked Mr Kenyon.

'Very sad,' I agreed.

He continued 'Sir, Her Highness left a Will wanting her body to be draped in her favourite sari for her cremation'. Whereupon he undraped the parcel in his hand and unfolded a most gorgeous purple silk sari with gold borders. 'You see sir, though we have wide experience in dressing bodies of the departed, we've never handled a sari. So I came to India House to get guidance on how a sari is draped round a lady's body. Perhaps you can help us'.

I could not resist blurting out: 'I am sorry Mr Kenyon, although I have some experience of taking them off, I have never put one round a lady'.

Mr Kenyon was shocked at my reply and walked out of my office carrying the parcel with him. He went straight to my boss to complain of my indecorous behaviour. A little later Krishna Menon sent for me and rasped: 'Sardar, can't you resist the temptation to show off your wit on the most unsuitable occasions?' Then he broke into a large smile. By the afternoon he had told everyone in India House of what I had said to Mr Kenyon of Kenyon and Kenyon Undertakers.

I could relate many similar episodes in my life but this is not the place for them. Since some of them relate to encounters with women and about drinking, I have been affixed with the label 'dirty old man of Delhi'. I belong to Delhi and am old (eighty seven) but I am not really dirty: I only like to tell dirty jokes.

I am not sure if there will be yet another compilation of my jokes. I hope others will take it up after I have been summoned by the Lord to regale Him with the latest jokes doing the rounds in the world He created.

January 13, 2002
New Delhi

DEATH RATES

Santa and Banta were close friends. Santa died suddenly. A desolate Banta went to the office of the local paper to put an announcement in its obituary column. He found their rates very high. So he decided to make it as short as he could—just two words: 'Santa dead.'

The clerk at the counter refused to take it. 'You must make it at least five words,' he told Banta.

'Okay,' replied Banta, and made it into five words: 'Santa dead. Maruti for sale.'

Contributed by Illoosh Ahluwalia, New Delhi

ELECTION SYMBOL

Banta told Santa, 'I am going to stand for election to the *Lok Sabha*. My election symbol will be a donkey.'

'Banta, there should be some difference between you and your election symbol,' replied Santa.

Contributed by J.P. Singh Kaka, Bhopal

WHAT A LIFE!

 Mr Saxena appeared before the judge to seek divorce from his wife. 'How old are you?' asked the judge.

'Thirty-five,' said Mr Saxena.

The judge noted his greying hair and wrinkled cheeks. 'May I see your birth certificate?'

Mr Saxena handed over his birth certificate.

'But Mr Saxena,' said the judge furiously, 'according to your certificate you are not 35 but 50 years old.'

'Your Honour,' replied Mr Saxena, 'I'm not counting the last 15 years I spent with my wife. You call that a life?'

Contributed by Shashank Shekhar, Mumbai

BRAYING COMPETITION

 Banta scolded his son: 'You are a donkey.' His son replied, 'But *Dadaji* (grandfather) called me, "*Tum gadhey key bachchey ho.*"' (You are the son of a donkey.)

Contributed by J.P. Singh Kaka, Bhopal

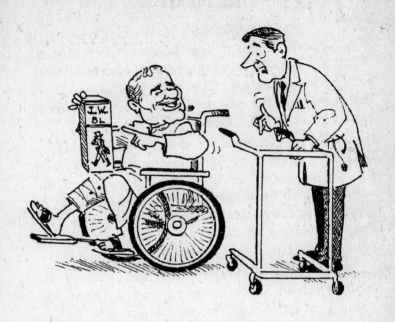

POST-OPERATIVE MEDICINE

After Prime Minister Vajpayee had his knee surgery, Dr Ranawat advised him: 'Sir, for a few days you will have to use a walker.'

'That is no problem, doctor. Will Johnny Walker be okay?'

Contributed by R.S. Mathur, Delhi

THE SILENCER

F.E. Smith, who later became Lord Birkenhead, was famous for his acidic wit and devilish sense of humour. When he was attending a luncheon in Swansea to mark the opening of the new town hall, he found himself sitting next to the Prince of Wales.

They both had to sit through a long-winded speech by the mayor, which never seemed to end. F.E. Smith picked up a menu card, wrote a few words on the back, and asked the toastmaster to give it to the speaker. Shortly after he had done this, the mayor made some closing remarks and sat down.

The Prince of Wales, who had noticed the incident asked Smith what he had written. 'Oh, nothing much,' Smith replied. 'I just told him his fly buttons were undone.'

Contributed by Judson K. Cornelius, Hyderabad

HONEYMOON PROBLEM

Santa's daughter Pammy was to be married. But as the wedding day drew closer, she grew more nervous. This was noticed by her mother who asked her the reason.

'It's the thought of going away on the honeymoon with him that's worrying me,' replied Pammy.

'Don't let that bother you,' assured her mother, 'I went on my honeymoon after I got married. So it's no big deal.'

'Ah, it was all right for you. *Tusi papaji naal gaye see.*' (You went with *Papaji.*)

Contributed by Shashank Shekhar, Mumbai

DARWIN ON EVOLUTION

Some children take after their fathers. Others look like their mothers and maternal uncles. Darwin's theory of evolution does not explain one phenomenon quite cogently. 'What I am looking for, is a principle by which we can tell why some children look like their neighbours!'

Contributed by Maj. Gen. Surjit Singh, Kolkata

DURAND LINE HUMOUR

The latest political anecdote from Islamabad. A Swiss, a Japanese, a Pakistani and an Afghan are travelling to Europe by ship. The others ask the Swiss the time and find that his Swiss watch is five minutes slow. The Swiss throws his watch overboard muttering, 'There are more at home.' They then switch on the TV, which is kaput. The Japanese throws it overboard muttering the same thing. The Pakistani then picks up the Afghan and throws him overboard.

Contributed by Biju Cherian, Hubli

TIT FOR TAT

A man got into an argument with the famous Urdu satirist, Kanhaiya Lal. Tempers rose. To end the dialogue Kanhaiya Lal said, 'I thought you were a gentleman.'

The other retorted, 'I also thought you were a gentleman.'

'You were absolutely right,' said Kanhaiya Lal. 'It was I who was mistaken.'

Contributed by R.N. Lakhotia, New Delhi

DELHI POLICE, WITH YOU, FOR YOU

A competition was organised to evaluate the police organisations in different cities, and forces from many cities were invited to participate. The process of identifying the best police force was undertaken and five forces were shortlisted:

- The New York Police,
- Scotland Yard,
- Royal Canadian Mounted Police,
- The Melbourne Police and
- The Delhi Police (yes, our very own *Dilli* Police.)

The race for the world's best police force was on. For the play-off, the judges decided that a tiger would be set free in the nearby forest, and the team that caught the animal in the shortest time would be adjudged the best police force in the world.

The NYPD went first . . . caught the tiger in 30 minutes . . . Nothing to it!

Next, the Melbourne Police went and returned in 20 minutes with the tiger.

The Canadian Mounties followed and caught the tiger in 15 minutes.

Scotland Yard had the cat in the cage in 10 minutes flat.

Last, but not the least, came the turn of *apna* Delhi Police. They seemed the favourites as the tiger is native to India. The big cat was set free, and three *Jats* took off after it in a Maruti Gypsy.

All eyes were on the clock, in anticipation that the *jawans* of Delhi Police would catch the tiger in record time .

The minutes went by, 10, 20, 30 . . . soon it was an hour, and the crack force of Delhi Police was not back!

Three hours later, the judges decided to go in and take a look. After a brief search they arrived at a clearing in the jungle. This is what they saw:

A bear tied to a tree trunk, was being brutally beaten (the famous *lathi*) by the three men. The shouting could be heard over the cries of the animal, '*Bol! tu sher hai* . . . *Bol! tu sher hai*!!' (Confess that you are a tiger . . . confess that you are a tiger!!)

Contributed by Ramesh Wadhwa

18

CLINTON'S CHOICE

During his stay at the Oberoi Hotel in Mumbai, Bill Clinton was sitting in the hotel's coffee shop. He had a good look at the special menu created for him and ordered coffee.

'How would you like your coffee, sir?' enquired a waiter, specially trained to look after the VVIP.

'I would like my coffee just like my women— strong and sweet,' replied Clinton.

'But black or white, sir?'

Contributed by Shashank Shekhar, New Mumbai

ON THE MOVE

A *sticker on a Maruti Baleno in Mumbai:*
'Laugh at your problems — everyone else does!'

Seen in a pub in Bangalore:
'Avoid hangovers — stay drunk!'

A *traffic slogan on a hoarding in Mumbai:*
'If you take one for the road, your car may be lying with "bottoms up" on that road!'

A *sign at a lady doctor's clinic in Meerut city:*
'Specialist in women and other diseases!'

Contributed by Shashank Shekhar, Mumbai

DOCTOR'S BILL

Banta's wife was complaining to her doctor that his bill was unreasonably high. 'Don't forget,' he reminded her, 'that I made 11 visits to your home while your son had the measles.'

'And why do you forget,' she countered, 'that he infected the whole school.'

Contributed by A.S. Deepak, Chandigarh

CROSS CONNECTION

 An urgent telephone call was made to General Musharraf by the Indian government prior to his visit to India. There was a lot of disturbance in the telephone lines between New Delhi and Islamabad. And the Indian spokesman said on the telephone to his Pakistani counterpart:

'Tell General Musharraf, an invitation has been extended to Hurriyat!'

Much to the surprise of the Indian government, Musharraf arrived in New Delhi much before the date of his expected arrival, thus upsetting all protocol. When Vajpayee asked Musharraf what had brought him so soon to India, Musharraf said: 'Well, it was you who had asked me over the phone to *hurry up*!'

Contributed by Priya Nath Mehta, Gurgaon

FACT AND OPINION

Maternity is a fact, paternity, an opinion.

Contributed by Maj. Gen. Surjit Singh, Kolkata

MONEY PROBLEMS

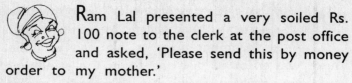 Ram Lal presented a very soiled Rs. 100 note to the clerk at the post office and asked, 'Please send this by money order to my mother.'

The clerk examined the soiled note and said, 'This is a tattered note, don't you have a better one to send to your mother?'

'It is my note, and it is my mother I want to send it to. What is your problem?' thundered Ram Lal.

Contributed by Ujagar Singh, Chandigarh

SIMPLE SCIENCE

Somebody once asked Einstein: 'Sir, what is this theory of relativity of yours?'

Pat came the reply: 'You keep your hand on a burning stove for a minute and you will feel as if one hour has passed. You spend an hour with a beautiful girl and you will feel as if only one minute has gone by. This is relativity.'

Contributed by Jasbir Singh, Jaipur

WHY MISS PAKISTAN WASN'T THE MISS WORLD

1. There was no Miss Pakistan.
2. Her family didn't allow her to wax her legs for the swimsuit competition.
3. She was 'honour-killed' on her way to the hotel.
4. Her *burqa* didn't turn the judges on.
5. Indian intelligence had her knocked off.
6. The Jews had her replaced by Suzy the Lahore Zoo elephant.
7. There was no flabby thighs contest.
8. The judges hadn't heard *Jhannjar phabdi na mutiar binna*.
9. She showed her a guitar as her 'favourite g-string'.
10. We sent a *hijra*.

Courtesy: The Friday Times, Lahore

UNIVERSAL PHENOMENON

Young son: 'Is it true, Dad, that in some parts of Africa a man doesn't know his wife until he marries her?'

Dad: 'That happens in every country, son.'

Contributed by Amir Tuteja, Washington

NAG PATI

Sometime back, my wife, Savinder, offered me a glass of milk. Generally I don't take milk, but on that day she compelled me to drink it. When I asked her why she was forcing me to take milk, she said: 'Aaj Nag Panchmi hai.'

Contributed by J. P. S. Kaka, Bhopal

CURE WORSE THAN THE DISEASE

The Supreme Court has sorted out Delhi's pollution problem. 'Buses must use CNG—all other fuels are banned.' This order created chaos, the public went through hell. The capital's air was cleaner, but it was left with plenty of woes.

Commuters were cursing: 'Oh, why can't we do what Mumbai's doing?' And what is Mumbai doing? Mounting one bus on another and cutting pollution in half.

Contributed by Rajeshwari Singh, New Delhi

Something Went Wrong in Jet Crash, Expert Says.

•

Safety Experts Say School Bus Passengers Should Be Belted.

•

Iraqi Head Seeks Arms.

•

Stud Tires Out.

•

Panda Mating Fails; Veterinarian Takes Over.

•

Soviet Virgin Lands Short of Goal Again.

•

Lung Cancer in Women Mushrooms.

•

Eye Drops off Shelf.

•

Squad Helps Dog Bite Victim.

•

Enraged Cow Injures Farmer with Axe.

•

Plane Too Close to Ground, Crash Probe Told.

•

Miners Refuse to Work after Death.

LET DOWN

Out of sheer *deshbhakti* (patriotism), Banta once tried his luck in the defence forces. He was an 'under trainee' for his first parachute jump. His sergeant was giving instructions: 'You count to ten and then pull this cord. If the parachute fails to open, you pull the emergency parachute cord here. And then try to land near the lorry down there, they will have a nice cup of tea waiting for you.'

Banta was flown high above the clouds and then let loose. He counted to ten and pulled the cord. Nothing happened. In a desperate bid, he pulled the emergency cord. Again, nothing happened. As he hurtled towards the lorry, he was heard to mutter: '*Mainon lagda hai ki thale chaa ve nahin milni!*' (I bet there's no cup of tea either!)

Contributed by Gagan Dhir, New Delhi

26

THE THIRD UMPIRE

I cannot rest, I cannot sleep,
    When Kapil cries, the heavens weep,
Kapil the beloved, noble, great
    Kapil in such a shattered state!
When money is the third umpire
    And the fate of a match is known already,
When gentleman has yielded place
    To the gambler and the greedy,
When mad excitement, palpitation, pride
    And the business of life shut beside
In the floodlight of match-fixing
    Look such a foolish thing,
When Wasim Akram and Hansie
    Still composed, still so fussy,
When so many without a sign of grace
    Fend it off with a straight face,
This must be said in his defence
    That Kapil still has a conscience.

Contributed by Kuldip Salil, Delhi

LOYALTY REWARDS

Emily Gloria Swanson remained a housekeeper of the family of John Kenneth Galbraith for more than forty years, managing his household affairs, rearing his children, accompanying his family to India and eventually attending to his grandchildren. Her character and devotion were illustrated one afternoon in the mid-1960s.

It had been a tiring day, and Galbraith and his wife had to get to a dinner. Galbraith asked Emily to hold all telephone messages while he had a nap. Shortly thereafter, the phone rang. President Lyndon Johnson was calling from the White House and he came on the phone himself. 'Give me Ken Galbraith. This is Lyndon Johnson.'

'He is sleeping, Mr President. He said not to disturb him.' When Johnson insisted on talking to her boss, she replied: 'No, Mr President, I work for him, not you.'

When Galbraith called the President back, Johnson could scarcely control his pleasure. 'Tell that woman I want her here in the White House.'

Contributed By Judson K. Cornelius, Hyderabad

GIFT OF A WIFE

The year 1946. World War II had ended. The British I.C.S. steel frame had softened and the British Officers were in a relaxed and friendly mood towards Indian officers. A very easygoing young I.C.S. official, Hibbert, happened to be the D.C. Kangra, who treated my father, late Lok Nath Bajaj, as an advisor rather than a subordinate officer. On March 31, 1946, my father sent a big heap of files for Hibbert's signatures, and hidden somewhere in the files was a single sheet memo seeking his approval. It read:

'If approved, Mrs Hibbert be married to me.'

Unsuspecting, Hibbert fell headlong in the trap and signed on the dotted line. Next day, on April 1, when my father confronted the D.C. with his orders, Hibbert was not found wanting in his sense of humour:

'Mr Lok Nath Bajaj, I have already had enough of her. I am happy she has some takers.'

Contributed by Jai Dev Bajaj, Pathankot

30

PARADOXICAL LAND

Isn't it a paradox like 'a graceful witch?'
  India is a poor country inhabited by the rich.
Go and see a scamster's abode
  You will find it glittering with gold.
Raid in a bureaucrat's house unearths a crore
  In a minister's house it yields even more.
Police and tax officers all roll in wealth
  Customs and excise chiefs enjoy better health.
Film stars, mafia dons and liquor kings
  Are multi-millionaires having diamond rings.
Who is poor? You and me
  Whom Big B is trying to make *crorepati*.

Contributed by G.C. Bhandari, Meerut

31

SAFE BUT...

 One day Santa was walking down a busy road when he realised a truck was headed right towards him.

Trying to be on the safe side he moved off the road, out of harm's way, but the truck veered right towards him.

Scared, Santa jumped into the bushes to avoid the truck. As the truck passed by, he stood up and started crying.

People gathered around and asked him why he was crying when the truck had missed him.

Santa replied that he was crying not because the truck had missed him, but because behind the truck was written—'*Phir Milenge!*' (We will meet again!)

Contributed by S Balagopalan, Hyderabad

JYOTISHI AND HIS PREDICTIONS

A palmist went to Ram Lal's house, where Ram Lal's wife had delivered a baby. He saw the baby's hand and predicted: 'This child will become the Rani of Jhansi.'

Ram Lal: 'But *Maharaj*, this is a boy.'

Palmist: 'Then he will become another Maharana Pratap.'

Contributed by J.P. Singh Kaka, Bhopal

CRICKET ANYONE?

 Santa said to Banta, "Come Banta, let's bet on the cricket match and make a lot of money".

Banta agreed, "Very true, *yaar*, let us bet on India."

So they both vouched for India and bet a good sum. After the match was over Santa lamented, 'My bad luck is always *kharaab yaar*, India lost the match and I lost my money."

Banta replied, 'There is still hope for me. I bet on the highlights also."

Contributed by Vijay Mewada, Mumbai

THE REASON WHY ...

'Papa, when Shri Ram*ji* was sent to exile for 14 years, why did Sita*ji* choose to go with him and not stay on in Ayodhya?' asked JP's son Gangadeep.

'Because she wanted to be with her husband,' Jp replied.

His wife pitched in: 'The real reason was she did not want to live with three mothers-in law.'

Contributed by J.P. Singh Kaka, Bhopal

MANUAL LABOUR

Once Dr C.E.M. Joad was being escorted through one of the major motor car factories in Detroit, where even humans appeared like automata. Dazzled by so many mechanical operations, he was taken to the restaurant where even the food was served automatically.

On the way out of the factory, Dr. Joad was descending in the elevator with his escort when one of the factory hands, also a passenger, pinched a female passenger. The young woman reacted indignantly. But Dr Joad rejoiced.

'Thank God,' he cried, 'that something is done by hand in this factory!'

Contributed by Judson K. Cornelius, Hyderabad

OF OUR TIMES...

There is an apt saying, pertinent to our times: *'Haanji kee naukari, naanji kaa ghar.'* (A job for one who says yes sir, one who says no sir stays at home.)

Contributed by Rajbir Deswal, Kanpur

Contraceptive:

A device which should be worn on every 'conceivable' occasion.

Neighbours:

The only people who listen to both sides of an argument.

Genius:

A guy who can do anything but make a living.

Marriage:

A ceremony in which rings are put on the finger of the lady and through the nose of the gentleman.

Bachelor:

A guy who never quite gets over the idea that he is a thing of beauty and a boy forever!

Contributed by Shashank Shekhar, Mumbai

HEAVEN AND HELL

 Heaven is to have an American salary, British House, Chinese food and an Indian wife.

Hell is to have an American wife, British food, Chinese house and an Indian salary!

Contributed by Narinder Singh, Calcutta

TAKEN FOR A RIDE

 A slightly befuddled Banta came out of a local bar and noticed a taxi. He went round and round and finally got in.

'Take me to Paharganj,' Banta told the driver.

'You are in Paharganj,' replied the driver.

'Thank you,' said Banta. 'Here's the money, and next time please don't drive so fast.'

Contributed by Shivtar Singh Dalla, Ludhiana

WITH THE TIMES

 Mrs Patel was justifiable uspset with the milkman for increasing the price of the milk.

'You add large quatities of water, and yet you have the audacity to increase the price of the milk,' she bellowed aggressively.

The milkman's reply stumped her. 'Madam, earlier I used tap water. With no one willing to trust municipal water, I too have started using mineral water.'

Contributed by K. Srinivasan Kaushik, Bellary

US OR THEM

Once there was a meeting of all Punjabi freedom fighters. They were planning for a free Punjab. Santa raised a point, 'Oh, we'll get Punjab from India, but how would we develop it?'

That was a difficult question indeed. Suddenly, Banta replied, 'No problem! We'll attack the USA, it would take us over and then we would be a state of the USA and we'll automatically get developed.'

All the *sardars* were happy with this very simple solution, but an old *sardar* did not utter a single word. Someone asked him why he wasn't happy. He replied, 'Oh! that's all right, but what would happen if by chance we take over USA?'

Contributed by Roshan Lal, Panaji

THE RIGHT NAME

A beauty parlour which opened here this week is named—*Leepa poti.*

Contributed by O.P. Bajaj, Jabalpur

WORLD'S LAZIEST MAN

 On being called to see the 'World's Laziest Man', the representative of the Guinness Book was surprised to be shown a man sleeping on top of a tree.

'If he climbed the tree to sleep, how can he be the world's laziest man?' the Guinness representative asked.

'He did not climb the tree, sir,' the man who had called him replied. 'Ten years ago he went to sleep on the ground not knowing that there was a seed beneath him.'

Contributed by Rajeshwari Singh, New Delhi

SERVING TWO MASTERS

A man once challenged Mark Twain to quote some passage from the scriptures forbidding polygamy.

'Certainly,' replied the humorist, 'No man can serve two masters.'

Contributed by B. Bhanu Prasad, Bellary

38

NOT SO LETHAL

 Burglars broke into Banta's house on *Diwali* night. Gathering courage Banta picked up his son's pistol and shouted, 'Hands up.' The burglars put up their hands. Banta gave them a sound thrashing while holding the pistol in one hand.

Hearing their cries for mercy Banta's son woke up and ran to help his father. 'Papa, papa, you won't know how to use this pistol,' he said. 'First fill it with water then press the trigger.'

Contributed by Madan Gupta 'Spatu', Chandigarh

TO PRAY OR NOT TO PRAY

 Ujaagar was quite sick of visiting the gurudwara every Sunday to offer *ardaas*. He once asked the head *Granthi*, 'Why should I pray when I don't feel like it?'

The *Granthi* replied, 'Pray when you feel like it, because *Wahe Guru* will bless you; pray when you don't feel like it, because that is when you need it most.'

Contributed by Gagan Dhir, New Delhi

NAME CALLING

The world's most avid cricket fan, Banta Singh, had arrived early at the stadium for the first one day international, only to realise that he had left his ticket at home.

Not wanting to miss any of the match, he went to the ticket booth and got in a long queue for another seat. After an hour's wait he was just a few feet from the booth when a voice called out, 'Hey, Balwinder!' He looked up, stepped out of the queue, and tried to locate the owner of the voice . . . with no success.

He realised he had lost his place in the queue, and had to go back to the end of the line and wait all over again. After he had purchased his ticket, he was thirsty, and went to buy a Coke. The line at the counter was also very long. But since the game hadn't started he decided to wait. Just as he got to the counter, a voice called out, 'Oye, Balwinder!' Again Banta got out of line looking for the owner of the voice. But with no luck.

He was very upset as he got back in line for his Coke. Finally he had his Coke and took his seat, eager for the game to begin. As he waited for the game to start, he heard the voice calling, 'Hey, Balwinder!' once more. Furious, Banta Singh stood up and yelled at the top of his lungs, 'My name is not Balwinder!'

Contributed by T. Balaji, Chennai

MACAULAY ON RECORD

Macaulay, whose infamous note on Indian scholarship rankles Indian minds to this day, was not highly regarded by his English colleagues. In his biography of Macaulay, Trevelyan quotes Sydney Smith's opinion: 'Yes, I agree he (Macaulay) is certainly more agreeable since his return from India. His enemies might perhaps have said before (though I never did so) that he talked rather too much; but now he has occasional flashes of silence that make his conversation perfectly delightful.'

Contributed by Deeraj Jha, Jhansi

RUN, MOUSE, RUN

A jackal saw a mouse running out of a jungle. He asked him what had transpired to make him run for his life. The mouse replied: '*Sher ki bebe kise nai chher di, aur shak meyrey pai ho rahya sai.*' (Someone made a pass at the tiger's sister and suspicion has fallen on me.)

Contributed by Rajbir Deswal

42

POWER CUT

 Two families were settling the terms and conditions of a matrimonial alliance. The bride's representative asked: 'What make of fridge would you like?'

The bridegroom's uncle replied: 'We possess the latest brand.'

'Microwave oven?'

'We already have one.'

'TV?'

'We have theatre-size.'

'What about an AC?'

'Do not worry. By God's grace we have all electrical gadgets.'

'Then what should we give with our daughter?' asked the worried father.

The bridegroom's father replied, 'Just give us a generator to run all these items.'

Contributed by Madan Gupta 'Spatu', Chandigarh

REMEMBERING C.R.

When C. Rajagopalachari as Prime Minister of the Old Madras Presidency was invited to address the students union of Presidency College, Madras, in 1937, young Aga Shahi, who later won a place in the ICS and opted for Pakistan, was president of the students' union. Welcoming *Rajaji* (as he was affectionately called), he concluded his address with these words: 'We extend a most respectful welcome to *Rajaji* who is socially, morally, politically and matrimonially connected to the Mahatma.' There was thunderous applause for Agha Shahi's speech.

Rose the most potent, grave and revered C.R. to reply: 'My dear young college union president and friends, thank you for the kind welcome. Somebody got a wife, somebody got a husband, but I was not the beneficiary.'

Contributed by Krishna Narayan, Cochin
(N.B. C.R.'s grand-daughter was married to
Mahatma Gandhi's grandson)

BETWEEN HUSBAND AND WIFE

● My wife dresses to kill. She also cooks the same way.

— *Henry Youngman*

● My wife and I were happy for twenty years. Then we met.

— *Rodney Dangerfield*

● A good wife always forgives her husband when she's wrong.

— *Milton Berle*

● I was married by a judge. I should have asked for a jury.

— *George Burns*

● The secret of a happy marriage remains a secret.

— *Henry Youngman*

Contributed by Amir Tuteja, Washington

GRATEFUL RAM LAL

 Having lost his donkey, Ram Lal got down on his knees and started thanking God. A passerby asked, 'Your donkey is missing; what are you thanking God for?'

Ram Lal replied, 'I am thanking Him for seeing to it that I wasn't riding the donkey at that time; otherwise I would have been missing too.'

Contributed by Sonia Advani, Mumbai

TALIBANS ALL

If your faith is blind
       And you are senile in the mind,
You will find with God's grace
       That the world is a wonderful place.
If you can fell and kill
       An infidel at will,
If you can hide your women underground
       And be culturally pure and sound,
You are definitely *jannat* bound.
       So we have decided to thrash
A birthday or a New Year bash
       And slay
       The Valentine's Day.
And crash into every honeymooner's bed
       Lest it should be said
That they have built a heaven on earth
       And we have lagged behind.
So from today, while we embrace the USA,
       No 'hello', no 'hi!'
We ban all merriment, all joy.
       And be one up with the Taliban State
To make our *Bharat* once again great.

Contributed by Kuldip Salil, Delhi

WHAT'S IN A NAME?

 President Clinton: 'I am sorry to say, Mr Sharif, that what you are doing in Kargil is not very *sharif*.'

Nawaz Sharif: 'Mr President, names have no bearing on political behaviour. Do you think what your Madeleine Albright has been doing in Kosovo makes her all that "bright"?'

Contributed by Tilak Rishi, Aravali Vihar

GERNAL KNOWLEDGE

QUESTION 'Why is it that boys always ask for a girl's hand and never her foot?'

Answer: 'Because on her hand she has gold rings, gold bangles and maybe a gold-plated watch as well, whereas on her feet all she has are high-heeled shoes or sandals.'

Contributed by Rajeshwari Singh, Delhi

GANDHI'S LAMENT

Well done, my sons.
 Burn the churches, attack the nuns,
Swell your cheeks and thump your chest,
 That is the answer to conversions.
I am sorry, all my life
 I preached truth, preached non-violence,
Foolishly preached religious tolerance,
 Fasted for peace and vainly died.
But I am glad now to see you triumph,
 Glad to see your sense of pride,
Keep up the good work, my dear sons
 And let this in my home be done.
In fundamentalism and bigotry
 Let us second to no one be,
Emulate the greatest in the field
 And push back this country,
Like our neighbour,
 Into the fourteenth century.

Contributed by Kuldip Salil, Delhi

THE JEALOUS HUSBAND

Jealous Banta hired a private detective to check on the movements of his wife. He wanted more than a written report; he wanted a video tape of his wife's activities.

A week later, the detective returned with a tape. They sat down together to watch it. Although the quality was less than professional, Banta saw his wife meeting another man! He saw the two of them laughing in the park. He saw them enjoying themselves at an outdoor cafe.

He saw them dancing in a dimly lit nightclub. He saw the man and his wife participate in a dozen activities with utter glee.

'I just can't believe this,' Banta said, distraught.

The detective said, 'What's there not to believe? It's right up there on the screen!'

Banta replied, 'I can't believe that my wife could be so much fun!'

Contributed by Akhtar Amani, Vijaywada

P FOR PAKISTAN

A visitor from Pakistan was taking a stroll in Nehru Park, enjoying the greenery and the flowers. He needed to empty his bladder but could not find a urinal. He could hold out no longer and went behind the bushes. Just as he was undoing his fly buttons, a policeman caught him. 'What do you think you are doing?' demanded the constable.

'I want to pee,' replied the visitor. 'I am from Pakistan and I don't know where to go. Please help me out.'

'Okay, follow me,' ordered the constable. 'I'll show you a place across the road with more greenery and flowers. You can pee there as much as you like.'

So the constable took him across the road to a garden, greener and more full of flowers than Nehru Park. The Pakistani emptied his bladder, thanked the constable and asked, 'Whose garden is this?'

'*Bhai Sahib*, this is the garden of the Pakistan High Commission.'

Contributed by G.S. Boela, New Delhi

POLITICAL SLOGANS

A multi-party group of political workers used to go for a morning walk in the vicinity of a small town. One day they passed by an ancient temple where a few devotees were chanting in a subdued voice, 'Bolo Jai Jai Krishna Murari.'

Hearing their chant, the BJP worker said, 'I guess they are singing, "Desh ka neta Atal Bihari."'

'No', remarked the Congressman, 'The refrain of their bhajan is "Sonia hai sartaj hamari."'

The BSP activist asserted, 'I believe they are humming "Mayawati ki maya niari."'

Discounting their surmises, the SP worker blurted: 'All of you are wrong. They are chanting "Mulayam maare chot karari."'

Contributed by G.C. Bhandari, Meerut

TWO FOR THE ROAD

On a Maruti van in Pune:

'Love thy neighbour, but make sure his wife doesn't get to know!'

On a Tata Sumo in Meerut:

'Make love not war—marry and do both!'

Contributed by Shashank Shekhar, New Mumbai.

FLY AT YOUR OWN RISK

From a Southwest Airlines employee: Welcome aboard Southwest Flight 276, Austin to Texas. To operate your seat belt, insert the metal tab into the buckle, and pull tight. It works just like every other seatbelt, and if you don't know how to operate one, you probably shouldn't be out in public unsupervised. In the event of a sudden loss of cabin pressure, oxygen masks will descend from the ceiling. Stop screaming, grab the mask, and pull it over your face. If you have a small child travelling with you, secure your mask before assisting with theirs. If you are travelling with two small children, decide now which one you love more.

Contributed by Zahina Shamail, Delhi

PREGNANT IDEA

Banto filled up her insurance form but left column No 5 'Whether you are pregnant or not' blank. The insurance underwriter scrutinised the form and wrote back to Banto, 'Please let us know whether you are pregnant or not, so that we may do the needful.'

Contributed by S. Chaudhary, Pehowa

IN ALPHABETICAL ORDER

A friend asked a lady: 'Why have you named your children VC, MC and ABC? Are you so enamoured of these decorations?'

The mother replied, 'No, not enamoured at all. The first one is named VC, because he was born out of a Virgin's Curiosity. The second is MC, because of Misplaced Confidence. The last one is because of Absolute Bloody Carelessness!

Contributed by P. B. Sarpeshkar, Bangalore

WELCOMING GENERAL MUSHARRAF

Seen on the back of an autorickshaw in Delhi:

Doodh mangogay to kheer deyngey
Kashmir mangogay to chir deyngey.

(Should you ask for milk, we will serve milk pudding, If you ask for Kashmir you will be rent apart.)

Contributed by Anil Kochhar, Delhi

STAFF MEMBER

 A group of eunuchs used to make purchases at Vinod Verma's general store. Upon the birth of his son, eunuchs stormed his house and after singing and dancing for about fifteen minutes demanded, Rs. 1,500 as *bakhshish*. Verma gave them Rs. 1,100, but the eunuchs insisted on getting the full amount demanded by them. When he flatly refused to yield to their demand, the leader of the eunuchs remarked, 'Well *babuji*, we shall give you a concession of Rs. 400. After all, you are our staff member.'

Contributed by G.C. Bhandari, Meerut

FISHING IN TROUBLED WATERS

A fisherman sitting on the river bank watched a beautiful girl undressing to take a swim. As she was about to dive in, he shouted: 'Swimming is prohibited here.'

'Why didn't you tell me before I took off my clothes?' she complained.

'Undressing is not prohibited,' he replied.

Contributed by Reeten Ganguly, Silchar

TIME HANGS HEAVY

An American who found himself in Moscow wanted to know the time. He saw a man approaching him, carrying two heavy suitcases and asked the fellow if he knew the correct time.

'Certainly,' said the Russian, setting down the two bags and looking at his wrist. 'It is 11:43 and 17 seconds. The date is Feb 13, the moon is nearing its full phase and the atmospheric pressure stands at 992 hectopascals and is rising.'

The visitor was dumbfounded but managed to ask if the watch that provided all that information was Japanese. 'No,' he was told, 'it is our own, a product of Soviet technology.'

'Well, that is wonderful, you are to be congratulated.'

'Yes,' the Russian answered, straining to pick up the suitcases, 'but these batteries are still a little heavy.'

Contributed by Raatim Firdausi, Ramgarh Cantt

KISSA CAPITAL KA

 Bihari Lal was bragging about his knowledge of state capitals. He proudly said, 'Go ahead, ask me, I know all of them!'

His friend said, 'O.K., which is the capital of Kerala?'

Bihari Lal replied, 'Oh, that's simple! K'

Contributed by Brij Mohan, Jabalpur

THE CHINESE CONNECTION

 Santa had a fourth child. He filled the columns on the birth certificate: 'Mother: Sikh. Father: Sikh. Kid: Chinese.'

'How come you write "Chinese" when both parents are Sikh?'

'Aah,' said Santa reading a newspaper. 'It says that every fourth person born on the earth now is a Chinese.'

Contributed by Usha Rao, Vijaywada

THE *KUMBH*

I have sinned all my life,
        If you don't believe me ask my wife.
Indulged in treachery, lechery, fraud,
        Ask my wife because she is a truthful lady.
She'll tell you how I am mean and greedy,
        And how I have missed the one and only
        opportunity
Of washing my sins as she has given me the slip
        And along with Sushma Swaraj and Sonia
        Gandhi
Has gone to *Sangam* to have a holy dip.
        She is bound to rise politically
And become a minister, maybe
        And be earthquake-free,
While I stand here high and dry,
        And for at least twelve years cry,
While she with all the past ones gone
        Is free to commit any new sin
And once again the holy pardon win.

Contributed by Kuldip Salil, Delhi

BEWARE OF *SAINIKS*

Thackeray's wild *sainiks*, who can dare?
> Cricketers and valentine sellers, they really scare.

To them, mosques and churches are un-Indian,
> But Michael Jackson is an exception!

They have an eye on baring beauty queens, so take care!

Contributed by M.G. Narasimha Murthy, Hyderabad.

65

TO CATCH A THIEF

Banta was shifting his residence. He was packing his belongings. By midnight he was tired and dozed off with the front door open. A sound woke him up. A thief was packing valuables. Banta found it very amusing; the thief was doing the job for him! 'When this smart guy finishes packing, I will catch him.'

Banta was a hefty guy; so when the burglar had finished packing, Banta jumped on him and tied him up. Then he went to the police station and reported the matter.

'What did you do to the thief?'

'I tied his hands; you come and collect him.'

'I hope you tied his legs too.'

Banta felt a chill down his spine; he had forgotten about the legs. He sat down for a while. Then he cheered up and said, 'Inspector *Saab*, the thief, he will still be there.'

'How do you know'?

'Well, that fellow is also a sardar.'

Contributed by S Namgyal, Sikkim

CIVILIANS *BULAO*!

The drought situation in the Thar and Balochistan areas of Pakistan was quite bad. The Army was sent in for relief work. The soldiers decided to dig a well. Lo and behold, they struck water. They immediately rang up General Pervez Musharraf and requested him to inaugurate the well. Unfortunately, when the General leaned over to see the water level, he fell into the well.

The soldiers lowered a rope and started pulling him out. However, the moment the General's head popped out of the well, being good soldiers they let go of the rope to salute him. With a big splash, General Musharraf was back in the well. This happened three times. The fourth time, as the soldiers were pulling him out, fearing the worst yet again, the General started to shout: 'Civilians *ko lao! Tum log mujhe bahar nahi nikal sakte.*' (Get some civilians. You chaps can't pull me out.)

Contributed by Kanchan Sharma, Delhi

SENSIBLE MARRIAGE

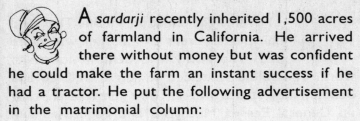

A *sardarji* recently inherited 1,500 acres of farmland in California. He arrived there without money but was confident he could make the farm an instant success if he had a tractor. He put the following advertisement in the matrimonial column:

'*Sardarji*, 40, recently arrived from Punjab wishes to marry woman, 30, owning tractor. Please send photo of tractor.'

Contributed by H. Kishie Singh, Chandigarh

OVER DRESSED

Wife: 'I need lots of new saris.'

Husband: 'But you already have over a hundred.'

Wife: 'I do, but the entire neighbourhood has seen all of them.'

Husband: 'I think it will be cheaper to move to a new neighbourhood.'

Contributed by Rajeshwari Singh, New Delhi

IT DOESN'T ADD UP

Teacher: 'If one woman does a job in one hour, how long, will it take for four women to do the same job?'

Student: 'Four hours!'

Teacher: 'Wrong! It will take them 15 minutes. You do not seem to know maths.'

Student: 'No, sir, it will take them four hours. You do not seem to know women.'

Contributed by Rajeshwari Singh, New Delhi

WHITE HOUSE HUMOUR

Question: Why did this young White House intern refuse to go for a course in sex-education?

Answer: Because she was told the final exam would be 'oral'.

Question: Why did this nymphomaniac take an intern's job at the White House?

Answer: Hoping to find sexual harassment in office!

Contributed by Shashank Shekhar, New Mumbai

COSTLY CLOCK

Banta came to Delhi. He was walking on a street which had a clock tower, when someone asked him if he wanted to buy the clock on the tower.

Banta said, 'Yes.'

'Give me a thousand rupees and I'll go get a ladder,' the man said.

The man took the thousand and disappeared.

Having waited for several hours Banta figured he had been taken for a ride.

The next day Banta was again walking along the same street and the same man asked him to buy the clock. 'Give me a thousand rupees and I'll go get a ladder.'

Banta put in his condition: 'I will give you a thousand rupees but I am not a fool. This time, you wait and I'll go get a ladder.'

Contributed by Priyanka Agarwal, Chandigarh

WELCOME TO DELHI

An English tourist arrived in Delhi and hired a taxi to take him for a tour of the city. He saw Parliament House and all the other buildings. To his astonishment, after a couple of minutes, he saw a second Parliament House and then a third one. Not realising that the driver was taking him past the same route again and again to extract the maximum money, he asked, 'In Britain, we have only one legislature building: how is it you have three?'

The taxi driver smiled and replied, 'Three? Five are yet to come, *Sahib*. Keep watching.'

Contributed by Vishnu Prasad, Kerala

ASTROLOGY AND JOSHIJI

Now you'll be able to know years in advance
  Whether your daughter will marry in
  Bhagalpur or France,

Whether your son'll become a doctor or a
  philosopher
  Or, stars favouring, a flourishing astrologer,

When your neighbour-woman is going to have
  labour pains,

By how much is the stock market going to crash.
  You'll know—in a flash
  The year and the month and the day of your
  luck

When you'll make a fast buck,
  How faithful your future wife will be,
Your children will know years in advance
  When you'll die
And plan accordingly.

  It is the proudest science of the 21st century
Congratulations, Dr Joshi,
  For introducing it at the university.

Contributed by Kuldip Salil, Delhi

72

SHORT 'N' SWEET

Bill Clinton landed in Mumbai, and in spite of his already hectic schedule, he was specially requested by a group of medical students to address a seminar on the subject of 'sex'.

Though Clinton was in a tearing hurry to leave for Hyderabad, he agreed to address the elite gathering. He arrived at the conference hall and made a six-word speech: 'Ladies and gentlemen, it gives me immense pleasure.'

Contributed by Shashank Shekhar, New Mumbai

ENGLISH LESSONS

A maid servant, who was learning English from the lady of the house, informed her telephonically, '*Mem sahib*, I'll not come for work today as I have got headache in my stomach.'

Contributed by J.P. Singh Kaka, Bhopal

FOUND... AND LOST

 Two friends, Santa and Banta, met at Chandni Chowk. Santa looked worried. 'What's wrong Santa?' asked Banta.

'I found two 100 rupee notes in the bus.'

'And you are not happy about it?'

'Actually, someone else saw them at the same time, so I had to share them.'

'A hundred rupees each. That's not bad!'

'No, it's not, but when I got home, I realised it was I who had lost the two hundred rupees in the first place,' declared Santa ruefully.

Contributed by Namita Saini, Jaipur

MISSING TAXI DRIVER

Magistrate: 'What was he doing when you arrested him?'

Policeman: 'He was arguing with a taxi driver, Your Honour.'

Magistrate: 'That is no proof he has drunk.'

Policeman: 'Well, Your Honour, there was no taxi driver there.'

Contributed by B. Bhanu Prasad, Bellary

TONGUE-IN-CHEEK

Women at different ages:

At 08 years:

You take her to bed and tell her a story.

At 18 years:

You tell her a story and take her to bed.

At 28 years:

You don't need to tell her a story to take her to bed.

At 38 years:

She tells you a story and takes you to bed.

At 48 years:

You tell her a story to avoid going to bed.

Contributed by Pulkit, New York

LICENCE RAJ

Ram Lal applied for a licence for a Bofors gun. On being asked why he had put in such an application, he said, 'I have asked for the licence for the Bofors gun because I knew you would reduce it to a licence for a revolver, this being a common practice in government offfices.'

Contributed by Rinki Yaqut

THE HISTORY LESSON

Banta was teaching history to his convent going son.

Jr. Banta: 'Dad, how do these wars begin?'

Banta: 'Well, son, suppose Pakistan has a quarrel with Japan, and . . .'

Mrs. Banta: 'But, Pakistan and Japan have never quarrelled.'

Banta: 'I know *bibi*—but I'm taking a hypothetical instance to . . .'

Mrs. Banta: 'But you are misguiding the boy.'

Banta: 'No, I'm not . . .'

Mrs. Banta: 'Yes, you are . . .'

Banta: 'I tell you, I'm not ! It's outrageous . . .'

Mrs. Banta: 'Shut up! You *bewkoof*.'

Banta: 'Mind your words or I'll . . .' (and gives her a slap.)

Jr. Banta: 'All right, dad, don't get excited, I think I understand better how wars begin.'

Contributed by Vikas Saini, Hissar

BALLE, BALLE!

A man had collected about 10 travellers around him in a train and was relating one Khushwant Singh joke after another. He decided to relate one *Sardarji* joke but just then he realised that he had a few listeners who were the typical strong and well-built Sikhs. So he changed the beginning from 'Once upon a time there was a *Sardarji*' to 'Once upon a time there was a *Bengali.*'

The five enraged *Sardars* picked him up and thrashed him to pulp, shouting throughout, '*Hum Sardar mar gaye kya?*' (*Sardar*'s are not dead yet!)

Contributed by Sucharit S. Rajadhyaksha, Pune

ADULTS ONLY

Why did 18 *Sardarjis* go to a movie?
Because below 18 was not allowed!!!

Contributed by Arshi Advani, Delhi

HAND OUT

An American, a Russian, a Frenchman and an Indian were travelling in an aeroplane for a world tour. A few hours after take off, the American stuck his hand out of the plane's window and declared that the aeroplane was cruising over America. The others asked him, 'How can you know that?'

The American replied, 'Simple'. Because of heavy industrial pollution my hand's complexion became black.'

After a few hours of journey the Frenchman said that the flight was over Paris as his hand had touched the Eiffel Tower. Later the Russian could recognise his country because of the cold, snowy weather.

Finally the Indian shouted loudly, 'Flying over India.' He explained that his watch had been stolen by someone when he had stuck his hand out.

Contributed by Irrinki Someshwara Rao

DONKEY *MEMSAHIB*

 In the days of the British Raj, an officer of Her Majesty's Government was holed up in a remote rural village. His child had caught chicken pox. No doctor was immediately available and hence he decided to implement his servant's advice.

The servant, after much effort, was able to explain to the Englishman that donkey's milk was a traditional remedy for the ailment. The Englishman ordered his servants to get hold of a donkey. Every time they got a donkey, it turned out to be a male one. Unable to explain in his broken Hindi that he wanted a female donkey and not a male one, he finally thundered, pointing to his wife, 'You fools, *mujhe memsahib jaisaa gadha chahiye.*'

Nothing is known of his wife's reaction!

Contributed by Sucharit S. Rajadhyaksha, Pune.

A LUCKY ACCIDENT

 Banta was hit by a vehicle. He shouted: 'Call the ambulance immediately.'
A pedestrian walking by replied: 'Don't worry, *Sardarji*, you were hit by an ambulance van.'

Contributed by J.P. Singh Kaka, Bhopal

OF CATS AND RATS

Banta was carrying a box under his arm as he walked down the street. Santa stopped him and asked, 'Oye, Bante, what's in that box?'

'A cat,' Banta said.

'What for?'

'Well, I'm going to drink and you know when I'm a bit tipsy, I see rats which frighten me. This cat will drive them away.'

'But,' Santa said wisely, 'those are not real rats.'

Banta snapped back, 'Bewakoof, this is not a real cat either.'

Contributed by Jitu Chanjmai, Jorhat

RESPONSIBILITY

A glimpse into Bihari Lal's school life. Young Bihari Lal to his father, who is reading his appalling end-of-term report: 'What do you think the trouble is, *Pitaji? Khaandaani ya swabhaavi.*' (Heredity or environment.)

Contributed by Gagan Dhir, New Delhi

ME TOO POLITICS

 At the Japanese Embassy in the USA, Prime Minister Mori was given some basic English conversation training before his meeting with President Bill Clinton. The instructor said, 'Mister Prime Minister, when you shake hands with President Clinton, please say: "How are you?" Then Mr Clinton will reply: "I am fine, and you?" To this you should say: "Me too." After that we translators will do all the work. It's quite simple.'

But when Prime Minister Mori met President Clinton, he mistakenly said: 'Who are you?'

Clinton was a bit shocked, but managed to react with humour, 'Well, I am Hilary's husband.'

At this, Prime Minister Mori confidently replied: 'Me too.'

Contributed by Somya Gupta, Jind

POLL VICTIM

'And how do you account for your recent defeat in the polls?'

'I was a victim.'

'A victim—of what?'

'Of accurate counting.'

Contributed by A. S. Deepak, Chandigarh

THE LALOO-JAYALALITHA DUET

Shut you up who call us corrupt
    And instead put up our bust
In every city-square, village and town
    And garland us, for our slogan now
Is down, down with corruption, down.

    Now, you, who call us corrupt
Before us bow
    For, though arrogance, greed and fraud is
    our creed,
We might have ruined our respective state,
    Nobody could ever accuse us of Defencegate.
You call us cunning, clownish, dirty
    But have we ever compromised this country's
    security?

We told you, we are innocent,
    And, cent per cent,
Compared to what you have seen
    On your TV screen
Ha, ha! We are snow-white clean.

Contributed by Kuldip Salil, Delhi

THE SMARTER BRAIN

In the hospital the relatives of the patient gathered in the waiting room, where he lay gravely ill. Finally the doctor came in looking tired and somber. 'I'm afraid I'm the bearer of bad news,' he said, as he surveyed the worried faces. 'The only hope left for your loved one at this time is a brain transplant. It's an experimental procedure, semi-risky, and you will have to pay for the brain yourselves.'

The family members sat silent as they absorbed the news. After a great length of time, someone asked, 'Well, how much does a brain cost?'

The doctor quickly responded, '$5,000 for a male brain, and $200 for a female brain.' The moment turned awkward. The men in the room tried not to smile, avoiding eye contact with the women, but some actually smirked.

A man, unable to control his curiosity, blurted out the question everyone wanted to ask: 'Why is the male brain so much more?'

The doctor smiled at his childish innocence and so to the entire group said, 'It's just standard pricing procedure. We have to mark down the price of female brains because they've been used.'

Contributed by Dhiren Joshi, Toronto

DIL MAANGE MORE...

A lady from Kerala moved into the house next door. She did her best to pick up Hindustani so that she could do her shopping unaided. She had not yet caught on to the difference between *pyaaz* (onion) and *pyaar* (love). When one morning she asked a vegetable hawker, '*Hum ko do kilo pyaar de sakta?*'(Can you give me two kilos of love?)

'*Behenji, sirf do kilo kyon?*' *Jitna maangey utna doonga.*' (Why only two kilos? I can give you as much as you want.)

Contributed by Anees Jung, New Delhi

HAIL HITLER!

'When will I die?' Hitler asked an astrologer.

'You will die on a Jewish holiday,' the tarot card reader forecast.

'Which one?' demanded Hitler.

'*Fuhrer*, any day you die will be a Jewish holiday,' the fortune teller said solemnly.

Contributed by Jitu Changmai, Jorhat

BE POSITIVE

Santa: 'Nurse, I am very eager to know my blood group.'

Nurse: 'B positive.'

Santa: 'Please tell me soon.'

Nurse: 'B positive.'

Santa: 'I am positive, but eager to know the blood group.'

Contributed by Anil Negi, Nainital

AWFULLY EXACT

Some tourists in the Museum of Natural History were marvelling at the dinosaur bones.

One of them asked Santa Singh, who was the guide showing them around, 'Can you tell me how old the dinosaur bones are?'

'They are three million, four years, and six months old,' replied Santa.

'That's an awfully exact number,' said the tourist. 'How do you know their age so precisely?'

Santa answered, 'Well, the dinosaur bones were three million years old when I started working here, and that was four and a half years ago.'

Contributed by Balkrishna Reddy, Guntur

GOLF

In Scotland, a new game was invented. It was entitled: Gentlemen only. Ladies forbidden.

And thus the word GOLF entered the English language.

Contributed by S.S. Shekhawat, Panchmarhi

INSTANT PREGNANCY

Banto boarded a crowded bus. Finding it difficult to bear the jolts, she requested a passenger to give up his seat to her because she was pregnant. The gentleman stood up and offered his seat to her. Standing by her side, he carefully examined her anatomy and felt cheated. He asked, '*Bahenji*, when did you become pregnant?'

'Only this morning,' replied Banto.

Contributed by Madan Gupta 'Spatu', Chandigarh

BUTTON UP

A Sunday *ardaas* (prayer) was on when suddenly the *Granthi* (priest) interrupted and decreed: 'A number of buttons have been found among the coins in recent collections. In future, please rend your hearts, and not your garments.'

Contributed by Gagan Dhir, New Delhi

HEAVEN OR HELL

'Did Shri Ram really suspect Sitaji of infidelity and subject her to *agnipariksha*?' asked the ever-inquisitive wife.

'I really don't know, but when I go to *swarg*, I'll ask him about it,' replied the husband.

'But what if because of all those hardships Shri Ram*ji* subjected Sita*ji* to, he is not in Heaven?' said the wife.

'In that case you can go and ask him yourself when you die,' quipped the husband.

Contributed by Shashank Shekhar, New Mumbai

HEAVY MAKE-UP

Banto: 'You are looking different today, Santo.'

Santo: 'Yes! The doctor advised me to reduce 5 kg.'

Banto: 'And you have reduced 5 kg?'

Santo: 'Yes! I have stopped putting on my make-up.'

Contributed by Rajeshwari Singh, New Delhi

NEVER TRUST A POLITICIAN

 A speeding bus-load of politicians hit a tree on the roadside, and all the passengers died. A farmer saw the accident, dug a hole and buried them all.

After a few days, a policeman came and asked the farmer whether he had seen the accident and if he knew where the politicians had gone. The farmer replied, 'Yes, I saw the accident, and as all the politicians had died, I buried them.'

The policeman asked, 'Were all of them dead?'

The farmer replied, 'Some of them said they were alive, but you know how these politicians are, they never tell the truth. I buried them all.'

Contributed by Lt Col P. B. Sarpeshkar (Retd.), Bangalore

BEWARE!

Sign in a domestic-appliances department: 'Going in for cheap water coolers may land you in hot water.'

Contributed by Savitri Bisht, Masoorie

WHEN GOD WENT MISSING

Two six-year-old boys attending religious school were giving the teacher problems. The teacher had tried everything to make them behave—timeouts, notes, punishment; but could do nothing with them. Finally, the boys were sent to see the priest. The first boy went in and sat on a chair across the desk from the priest. The priest asked, 'Son, do you know where God is?' The little boy trembled but said nothing. The priest leaned across the desk and asked again, 'Do you know where God is?' The little boy bolted out of the chair, ran past his friend in the waiting room and ran straight home. He got into bed and pulled the covers up over his face.

His friend, who had followed him home asked, 'What happened in there?'

The boy replied, 'God is missing and they think we did it!'

Contributed by Fazal-A-Esaf, Mumbai

PRICKLY ONE, THIS

Once a Hindu, a Muslim and our dear Santa were standing together. An Englishman came up and asked, 'Hey guys, what are your favourite flowers?

The Hindu replied, 'Lotus'.

'Ha, I clean my shit with that!' the Englishman jeered.

The Hindu was surprised and angry, the lotus being our national flower.

The Muslim replied: 'Chameli'.

'Ha, I clean my shit with that!' was the Englishman's response.

The Muslim was surprised and angry.

The Englishman asked Santa, '*Sardarji*, and what is your favourite flower?'

Patriotic Santa replied: 'Cactus! *Ab kar le saaf.*' (Now clean your ass).

Contributed by P. S. Gambhir, Indore

FAREWELL TO LALOO

Colours are splashing all around
    Because we have won new ground
In ethics, law and probity
    In Bihar
    In a pious and holy war.
Our star is democracy's glorious hour,
    Because we have built a new tower
To gubernatorial impartiality.
    It is an hour of pure glee
Because jungle Raj will cease to be
    And every criminal will now be free
To raise his price as never before.
    What more could you ask for?
For a state like Bihar
    Has now total peace and tranquillity.
Though it was a seven days' wonder,
    Let's celebrate Laloo's fall
And drown each other in *gulal*.

Contributed by Kuldip Salil, Delhi

THE BIG SQUEEZE

The local bar owner was so sure that his bartender was the strongest man around that he offered a standing $1000 bet. The bartender would squeeze a lemon until all the juice ran into a glass, and hand the lemon to a patron. And he who could squeeze one more drop of juice from it would win the money. Many people tried, weight lifters, longshoremen, etc., but nobody could do it.

One day a scrawny little man came in wearing thick glasses and a polyester suit, and said in a tiny, squeaky voice, 'I'd like to try the bet.'

After the laughter had died down, the bartender said, 'OK,' grabbed a lemon, and squeezed away. He then handed the wrinkled remains of the rind to the little man. But the crowd's laughter turned to total silence as the man clenched his fist around the lemon and six drops fell into the glass.

As the crowd cheered, the bartender paid the $1000, and asked the little man, 'What do you do for a living? Are you a lumberjack, a weight lifter, or what?'

The man replied, 'I work for the Internal Revenue Service (the Income Tax Department)'.

Contributed by Amir Tuteja, Washington

WHO'S THE BOSS?

Banta Singh was complaining at a staff meeting the other day that he wasn't getting any respect. Later that morning he went out and returned with a small sign that read, 'I'm the boss.' He then taped it to his office door.

Later that day when he returned from lunch, he found that someone had taped a note to the sign that said:

'Your wife called. She wants her sign back!'

Contributed by Amir Tuteja, Washington

NO *SUVIDHA*

Ram Lal married a girl who worked in the telephone exchange. On the first night, being tired the girl fell asleep as soon as she got into bed. When Ram Lal tried to wake her saying he wanted to make love, she sleepily replied, 'Sorry but this service is no longer available on this number.'

Contributed by Rajeshwari Singh, New Delhi

MODESTY UNCOVERED

The medium had aroused great interest throughout the crowded hall by reading a newspaper through a thick black cloth while blindfolded. The judges examined the bandage over his eyes and doubled the cloth over the newspaper, but he still read with ease anything placed before him.

At this point an old woman arose and started towards the door. 'You aren't leaving, are you?' inquired a friend.

'I am,' was the emphatic answer. 'This is no place for a respectable woman with a thin calico dress!'

Contributed by S. Viswanatha, Mandya

TO CATCH A BUS

A stranger asked a farmer if it was possible to reach the nearest bus stop in half an hour by taking a shortcut through the fields.

'Sure,' replied the farmer. 'And if the guard dogs see you, you might not even take fifteen minutes,' he added matter-of-factly.

Contributed by Jitu Changmai, Jorhat

CHICKEN THIEF

Judge: 'So you are charged with stealing a chicken?'

Santa: 'Yes, your honour.'

Judge: 'Where is your lawyer?'

Santa: 'I do not have one.'

Judge: 'Well, I will ask one to defend you.'

Santa: 'No, sir, please.'

Judge: 'Why not?'

Santa: 'Because I want to enjoy the *murga* myself.'

Contributed by B. Bhanu Prasad, Bellary

A KEY MISTAKE!

An inebriated Girdhari Lal was trying to open his flat by forcing a cigarette into the keyhole. 'It won't open the door,' Santa, his neighbour, pointed out to him.

Girdhari Lal took a look at the cigarette and said glumly, 'Huh! I must have smoked my key by mistake.'

Contributed by Jitu Changmai, Jorhat

INSPECTOR 'TROUBULL'

Banta challenged the stranger entering his farmland. With an air of great importance the visitor produced his card and remarked: 'I am a government inspector and am entitled to inspect your farm.'

Sometime later Banta saw the inspector running for all he was worth to get away from a bull that was chasing him. Leaning over the fence Banta shouted: 'Show him your card, mister—show him your card.'

Contributed by Shivtar Singh Dalla, Ludhiana

NAUGHTY THOUGHTS

A cute young woman was consulting a psychiatrist. Among other questions, the doctor asked, 'Are you troubled by indecent thoughts?'

'Why, no,' she replied, with just the hint of a twinkle in her eye. 'To tell you the truth, doctor, I rather enjoy them.'

Contributed by A. S. Deepak, Chandigarh.

OVERHEARD

 '*Bahen*, I have absolutely no faith in astrologers. Their predictions always prove wrong.'

'What happened?' asked her companion.

'See, I consulted an astrologer about my marriage. After going through my horoscope and reading my palm, he predicted that I would marry a handsome young man holding a high post at the age of 23.'

'But you must have been married to him a little later, isn't it?'

'*Na, Bahen*, I happend to marry the same old idiot at the age of 32!'

Contributed by Mamta Verma, Bareilly

HOW'S THAT?

If multiplication is the converse of division, how do amoebas multiply by dividing?

Contributed by Vivek Prasad, Kerala

MONARCHY VS DEMOCRACY

The political science professor was explaining the difference between monarchy and democracy. Elaborating on the subject, he said, 'The King is his father's son. The Prime Minister is not!'

Contributed by Maj. Gen. Surjit Singh, Kolkata

THE MISSING WIFE

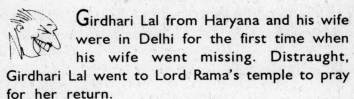

Girdhari Lal from Haryana and his wife were in Delhi for the first time when his wife went missing. Distraught, Girdhari Lal went to Lord Rama's temple to pray for her return.

From the side wall, Hanumanji beckoned to him and said, '*Ureaajaa molar, jab iski lugaaee kho gai thee to manney he tohi thee.*' (Foolish man, come to me. When Rama's wife was abducted, I helped him get her back.)

Contributed by Rajbir Deswal

STRANGER IN THE NEIGHBOURHOOD

An inebriated Banta came out of the bar as it was striking twelve on the clock in the the town square clock tower. He looked confused, and asked a passing gentleman, 'Badshaho, mennu eh daso, hon din de barah baje hai, ya raat de bara baje?' (Please tell me whether it is striking twelve of the day or night?)

The passerby stopped and mulled over the problem and said, 'Maaf karo ji, mai is ilake te nahi rehnda.' (I am sorry I don't know, I don't live in this area.)

Contributed by Lt Col P. B. Sarpeshkar (Retd.), Bangalore

MISFORTUNE

Banta decided to visit a fortune teller. 'You will be poor and unhappy until you are 30,' said the fortune teller, after examining Banta's palm.

'And then?' asked the eager Banta.

'Then you'll get used to it,' snapped the fortune teller.

Contributed by G.T. Vikram, Bangalore

CLASSIFIED GOOFS

Monday

For Sale: Mr Antony De'melow has one sewing machine for sale. Ph 5152431 after 7 pm and ask for Ms Leila who lives with him cheap.

Tuesday

We regret having erred in Mr. D'mellow's ad yesterday. It should have read one sewing machine for sale cheap ph 5152431 & ask for Ms Leila who lives with him after 7 pm.

Wednesday

Mr De'mellow has informed us that he has received several annoying phone calls because of the error in the classified ad of yesterday—it stands corrected as follows:

For Sale: Mr De'mellow has one sewing machine for sale. Cheap. Ph 5152431 after 7 pm and ask for Ms Leila who lives with him.

Thursday

I, Mr Antony De'mellow, have no sewing machine for sale. I smashed it. Don't call as I have had the phone disconnected. I have not been carrying on with Ms Leila. Until yesterday she was my housekeeper but she quit.

CAUGHT RED HANDED

Three guys—Banta, an Italian and a Jew worked together at a factory. Every day they noticed that their boss would leave work a little early. So one day they met together and decided they too would leave early that day if the boss did so.

As expected, the boss left before closing time and the three of them too left the factory early. The Jew went home and rested so that he could get an early start the next day. The Italian went home and cooked dinner.

Banta too reached home. He walked up to his bedroom, opened the door slowly to surprise his wife, only to see her in bed with his boss. He quickly shut the door and left.

The next day, the Italian and Jewish guys planned to go home early again and asked Banta if he too wanted to do the same. Banta said he wouldn't repeat it. The others asked the reason.

He replied, 'Because, yesterday I almost got caught!'

Contributed by Deepa Mathur, USA

Share a joke with Khushwant Singh

If you have a joke, a humorous anecdote or a funny incident, which is original and you would like to share it with Khushwant Singh and his million admirers, send it to us today. If selected, it would be printed in the next edition of Khushwant Singh's Joke Book.'

... and a million others

Remember

- Each joke or anecdote must be neatly typed or written on a separate sheet of paper in about 125-150 words.

- Do not type or write on both sides of the sheet. Write on one side only.

- Send your jokes to:

  Khushwant Singh's Joke Book
  c/o **Orient Paperbacks**
  Madarsa Road, Kashmere Gate,
  DELHI-110 006

- Each contribution received would be acknowledged.

- Each selected contribution would be acknowledged and included in the next edition of **Khushwant Singh's Joke Book** along with the name of the contributor.

Khushwant Singh's Joke Book

Entry Coupon

Name: ....

Address: ....

....

City .... Pin ....

Each entry must be accompanied by one coupon

✂

Khushwant Singh's Joke Book

Entry Coupon

Name: ....

Address: ....

....

City .... Pin ....

Each entry must be accompanied by one coupon

✂

Khushwant Singh's Joke Book

Entry Coupon

Name: ....

Address: ....

....

City .... Pin ....

Each entry must be accompanied by one coupon

A REASONABLE QUESTION

Teacher : 'Banta, tell me, where is Mount Everest?'

Banta : 'I don't know, Ma'am.'

Teacher : 'Stand up on the bench.'

Banta : 'Will I be able to see it then?'

Contributed by P. S. Ramesh, Bangalore

MATCH FIXING

Banta decided to make money by betting on cricket matches. He called a bookie and asked, 'How many cricket matches are there this month?'

'Ten,' was the answer, and he bet on all ten and lost them all.

The following month, he called the bookie, learned that there were 12 games and bet on all 12. Again he lost the whole lot.

A few months later, the unlucky Banta was on the phone again asking, 'How many cricket matches are there this month?'

'None,' answered the bookie. 'But I have several hockey matches coming up.'

'You fool,' cried Banta. 'What do I know about hockey.'

Contributed by G.T. Vikram, Bangalore

STATE SECRET

The president of a country was making a public speech. Somebody from the audience got up and said, 'Mr. President, you are an idiot.' He was immediately arrested and taken to the court of law.

The judge fined him 1,000 coins of the country. He pleaded not guilty and said, 'Sir, it is too much.'

The Judge replied, 'One hundred coins for insulting the president in public and nine hundred coins for disclosing a state secret.

Contributed by Dr O.P. Kapur, Sonepat

ORDER PLEASE

Ram Lal was brought to court on charges of drunken driving. Just before the trial there was a commotion in the gallery.

The judge pounded the gavel on his table and shouted, 'Order, order.'

Ram Lal immediately responded, 'Thank you, Your Honour, I'll have a Scotch and soda.'

Contributed by Kumar Surendra, Hazaribagh

CHOR, CHOR

Santa and Banta went to Pakistan on a trip. They were walking down the street in one of the poorer areas when a Pakistani on a bicycle raced by.

'What was that?' asked Santa.

'A thief,' replied Banta.

They walked on for a few minutes more when another bicycle raced by, this time with two Pakistanis on it.

'What was that?' asked Santa.

'Organised crime,' replied Banta.

Contributed by Gurpinder Singh Sohil, Ludhiana

THE ABC OF DEATH

Every time Ujaagar browses through the Obituary Columns, he thinks to himself, perplexed, 'Strange, how everybody seems to die in alphabetical order?'

Contributed by Gagan Dhir, New Delhi

DEMOLITION EXPERT

 A retired Madras Sapper Officer who had returned to the UK, had been employed as a Recruiting Officer during the war years. Enrolment of women into the Services was quite common. One day a prostitute volunteered for enrolment into the army. In one of the forms she had to fill, there was a column 'Employment Before Enrolment.' She did not want to write prostitute, as it embarassed her and she thought it was inappropriate. So she went to the Recruiting Officer for advice.

You may not know that Sappers construct roads, bridges and defences, and destroy those of the enemy. So this Sapper replied, without batting an eyelid, 'Please write, "Demolition of Temporary Erections."'

Contributed by Lt. Col. (Retd.) P. B. Sarpeshkar, Bangalore

PERFECT PATIENTS

Four surgeons were discussing the professions which make the best patients to operate on. The first surgeon said, 'I like to see accountants on my operating table because, when you open them up, everything inside them is numbered.'

The second responded, 'You should try electricians! Everything inside them is color coded.'

The third surgeon said, 'I really think librarians are the best; everything inside them is in alphabetical order.'

But the fourth surgeon shut them all up with this observation: 'You're all wrong. Politicians are the easiest to operate on. There's no guts, no heart, no spine, and the head and butt are interchangeable.'

Contributed by Somya Gupta, Jind

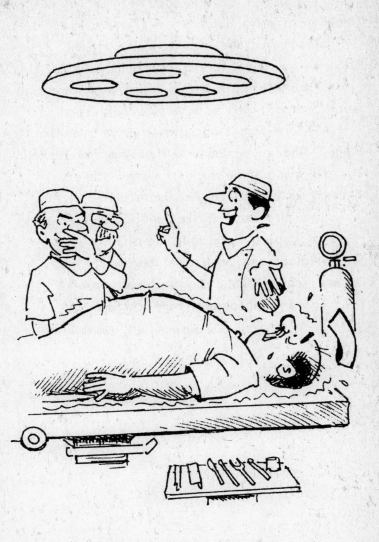

WISHFUL THINKING

Since air is pure and water is clean,
Since what we say we really mean,
Since we are honest and our dealings fair,
Dubious means aren't found anywhere.
Truth is our motto and service our creed,
We are free from the virus of greed.
Money—the government officials do not make
As bribe they do not a paise take.
Without graft, like an Arabian steed,
The files race at tremendous speed.
Head of department! don't be shy,
Without any hesitation, certify,
'In my department, I say with conviction,
There is absolutely zero corruption.'

Contributed by G.C. Bhandari, Meerut

SWEET SANTA

One day Santa rushed home and went straight to the kitchen. His wife saw him open the sugar container, look inside, close it, and keep it back. After some time, Santa again went to the kitchen, picked up the sugar container, opened it, peeped inside, closed it and kept it back. An hour later he did the same thing. Another hour and his wife saw him go through the same actions again.

Puzzled, she asked him the reason for his behaviour. 'Why are you opening the sugar container and looking inside so often?'

Replied Santa, 'I am a sugar patient you know... and the doctor advised me to check the sugar often.'

Contributed by Aditi Dayal, Ranchi

SURVIVAL TIP

What do you do when a *sardar* throws a hand grenade at you?

Pull the pin and throw it back.

Contributed by Jagdish Seth, Ludhiana

MARRIAGE *MASALA*

When a man steals your wife, there is no better revenge than to let him keep her.

•

I haven't spoken to my wife in 18 months—I don't like to interrupt her.

•

My girlfriend told me I should be more affectionate. So I got myself two girlfriends.

•

Man is incomplete until he is married. Then he is finished.

•

Then there was a man who said, 'I never knew what real happiness was until I got married; then it was too late.'

•

The trouble with being the best man at a wedding is that you never get to prove it.

•

Eighty per cent of married men cheat in America. The rest cheat in Europe.

•

Marriage is the triumph of imagination over intelligence. Second marriage is the triumph of hope over experience.

Contributed by Amir Tuteja, Washington

CANDID CANDIDATE

Santa applied for an engineering position in a multinational company office in Amritsar. Reddy from Hyderabad also applied for the same job. Both had similar qualifications and were asked to take a test.

The results showed that both had missed one question only. The manager went to Santa and said, 'Thank you for your interest, but we've decided to give the job to Mr. Reddy.'

Santa asked, 'And why would you be doing that? We both got 9 questions correct. This being Punjab I should get the job!'

The manager replied, 'We have made our decision not on the correct answers, but on the one question that you got wrong.'

'And just how would one incorrect answer be better than the other?' Countered Santa.

'Simple, for the question that both of you got wrong, Mr. Reddy put down, "I don't know" as the answer, and you wrote, "Neither do I"!'

Contributed by S Rangnathan, Mysore

THE GROOM WORE BLACK

Christina was about six or seven years old. She had gone to a wedding. While the bride and bridegroom were entering the church, Christina was surprised to see the bride in a pure white gown overflowing with frills, and a large hat with white flowers. So just out of curiosity, she asked her mother, 'Mommy, why the bride is always dressed in white?'

'Because white symbolises happiness. She wears it to show happiness on this day,' replied her mother.

To which Christina unhesitatingly responded: 'Oh, that is why the bridegroom is dressed in black.'

Contributed by Deepti Baliga, Mumbai

PRIDE AND POPULATION

We are more than a billion,
　　Still we are in slumber;
To hell with the quality of life,
　　We are proud of our number!

Contributed by G.C. Bhandari, Meerut

116

CULTURAL COURTESY

How do you think different people will react when you ask them — *'Kya mein aapko taklif de sakta hoon?'*

Probably like this —

Sardarji — *'Oye, zaroor malko!'*

Tamilian — *'Oyee-O! Magar kyoon ji?'*

Haryanvi — *'Deke to dekh!!'*

Contributed by Ankur Singh, Panchkula

WHAT'S UP, DOC?

Sherlock Holmes and Dr Watson were on a camping and hiking trip. They had gone to bed and were lying there looking up at the sky.

Holmes said, 'Watson, look up. What do you see?'

'Well, I see thousands of stars.'

'And what does that mean to you?'

'Well, I imagine it means we will have another nice day tomorrow. What does it mean to you, Holmes?'

'To me, it means someone has stolen our tent.'

Contributed by Sukhvinder Singh, Panipat

AGRA DISAGREEMENT

India hosted the summit in Agra
    And lavishly entertained the guest.
Admiring our food, Sehba said,
    'Your soup and *gosht* are the best.'
In Simla, we had a solemn pact,
    In Lahore, we signalled an agreement to tend.
What did we achieve in Agra?
    A disagreement from beginning to end.

Contributed by G. C. Bhandari, Meerut

THANK GOD

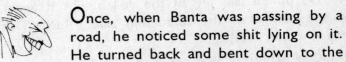 Once, when Banta was passing by a road, he noticed some shit lying on it. He turned back and bent down to the piece of shit and said, '*Chee!* this looks like shit.' Then he bent further down. After smelling it, he said, '*Cheeeee*, this smells like shit only.' Then he put his finger in it and after putting the same finger in his mouth he said, '*Chee*' this tastes also like shit.'

Finally, he got up and walked away saying, 'THANK GOD I DID NOT STAMP ON IT!!!!!'

Contributed by Mahaveer K, Bangalore

SOUND RESEARCH

Ujagar Singh was very keen on doing his Ph.D. He was in search of a subject on which no research had ever been done. One day, thinking about it, he saw a cockroach on the table in front of him. He immediately decided to undertake research on the roach.

He picked the roach and put it in the centre of the table and said: 'Run.' The roach ran.

He pulled off one leg of the roach, put it again in the centre of the table and said: 'Run.' The roach ran. He pulled one more leg off the roach, put it back on the table and said: 'Run.' The roach ran, even though it had just one leg.

He pulled last leg of the roach, put it again in the centre of the table and said: 'Run.' The roach could not!

Our professor was satisfied with his study and started on his thesis:

'When you pull out all the legs of a roach, it cannot hear anymore.'

Contributed by Ashok Sivanand, Bhopal

LEARNING ENGLISH

Indira Gandhi sent Buta Singh to England to learn English. On his return, she called him to her chamber and said, 'Mr. Singh, you've been abroad at the state's expense. I'd definitely like to know how well you've learnt the language. So please speak a few sentences.'

Buta Singh responded confidently; 'Madam, *main* capital letters *mein bolu ya* small letters *mein?*' (Madam, shall I speak in upper case alphabets or lower case?)

Contributed by Jitu Changmai, Jorhat

CHECK IT OUT

In a Yugoslav hotel:

The flattening of underwear with pleasure is the job of the chambermaid.

Sign in a Copenhagen airline ticket office:

We take your bags and send them in all directions.

In a Norwegian cocktail lounge:

Ladies are requested not to have children in the bar.

Advertisement for donkey rides in Thailand:

Would you like to ride on your own ass?

In a Rome laundry:

Ladies leave your clothes here and spend the afternoon having a good time.

In an Acapulco hotel:

The Manager has personally passed all the water served here.

On the faucet in a Finnish washroom:

To stop the drip, turn cock to right.

Contributed by Pulkit Advani, New York

THE HARRIED PHARMACIST

Upon arriving home, a husband was met at the door by his sobbing wife.

Tearfully she explained, 'It's the pharmacist. He insulted me terribly this morning on the phone.'

Immediately the husband drove downtown to confront the phamacist and demand an apology.

Before he could say more than a few words, the druggist told him, 'Now, just a minute, please listen to my side of it...

'This morning the alarm failed to go off, so I was late getting up. I went without breakfast and hurried out to the car, just to realise that I had locked the house with both house and car keys inside. I had to break a window to get my keys. Then, driving a little too fast, I got a speeding ticket.

'Later, about three blocks from the store, I had a flat tyre. When I got to the store there was a bunch of people waiting for me to open up. I opened and started waiting on these people, and all the time the darn phone was ringing off the hook.'

He continued, 'Then I had to break a roll of nickels against the cash register drawer to make change, and they spilled all over the floor. I got down on my hands and knees to pick up the nickels; the phone was still ringing. When I came

123

up I cracked my head on the open cash drawer, which made me stagger back against a showcase with a bunch of perfume bottles on it...all of them hit the floor and broke.

'Meanwhile, the phone is still ringing with no let up, and I finally got to answer it. It was your wife. She wanted to know how to use a rectal thermometer...and, honest, mister, all I did was tell her!'

Contributed by Kanchan Sharma, Delhi

INDUSTRIOUS DUO

A passerby watched two sardar's in a park. One was digging holes and the other was immediately filling them in again. 'Tell me,' said the passerby, 'what on earth are you doing?'

'Well,' said the one who was digging, 'usually there are three of us. I dig the hole, Balwant plants the tree and Ujaagar fills in the hole. Today Balwant is off ill, but that doesn't mean Ujaagar and I get the day off, does it?'

Contributed by Brahma Dev, Dehradun

IT'S A MAD, MAD, WORLD...

We are unable to announce the weather. We depend on weather reports from the airport, which is closed due to weather. Whether we will be able to give you a weather report tomorrow will depend on the weather.

— *Arab News report*

•

What good is the moon if you can't buy or sell it?

— *Ivan Boesky, Wall Street stock trader*

•

I have opinions of my own — strong opinions — but I don't always agree with them.

— *George Bush, US President*

•

Your pension will be stopped effective March 2001, because we received a notice that you passed away. May your soul rest in peace. You may reapply if there is a change in your circumstances.

— *Department of Social Services, South Carolina, USA*

TWO OR THREE

Banta and his newly married bride Banto were visiting friends when the topic of children came up.

The bride said she wanted three children, while the young husband said two would be enough for him.

They discussed this discrepancy for a few minutes, until Banta thought he'd put an end to things by saying boldly, 'After our second child, I'll just have a vasectomy.'

Without a moment's hesitation, the bride retorted, 'Well, I hope you'll love the third one as if it's your own.'

Contributed by Chhaya Rani, Dubai

TERRIBLE TRAGEDY

Did you hear about the latest tragedy in Punjab? There was a terrible power failure in a large shopping mall, and people were stuck on the escalators for four hours!

Contributed by Geetanjali, 24 Paragnas

OBEDIENT DADDY

A father of five came home with a toy, summoned his children and asked which one of them should be given the present.

'Who is the most obedient, never talks back to mother and does everything he or she is told?' he enquired.

There was a silence, and then a chorus of voices: 'You play with it, Daddy!'

Contributed by B. Bhanu Prasad, Bellary

THUS SPAKE THE BOY

Arriving at a small village, a priest asked a little boy for directions to the local church. The boy duly gave the directions.

'Thank you very much. I'd like you, your mummy, daddy and all your friends to come to the church tonight,' said the priest.

'What for?' asked the surprised boy.

'I'll be giving a sermon and want to tell you all how to find heaven,' explained the preacher.

'Don't make me laugh,' retorted the boy. 'You didn't even know where the church was.'

Contributed by Dharambir Taneja, Delhi

FAIR EXCHANGE

When Girdhari's buffalo strayed into the neighbour's field and ate up some of his wheat, the neighbour complained, to which Girdhari replied, 'Don't worry, tomorrow I will send you all the dung my buffalo yields from your crop.'

Contributed by Satinder Pal, Chandigarh

DOWRY GIRL

 Girl's father: 'My daughter sings so well that you will forget to listen to tape-recorders and stereos after you hear her. She dances so superbly that once you see her dancing, you will stop watching TV and the VCR. And she washes clothes better than any washing machine.'

Boy's father: 'But I have already accepted your daughter's hand for my son. So why are you telling me all this?'

Girl's father: 'So that you do not ask for these items as part of her dowry.'

Contributed by Rajeshwari Singh, New Delhi.

THAT SINKING FEELING

Santa bought his wife a new car. Two hours later she telephoned Santa frantically and said, 'There is water in the carburettor.' Santa was taken aback. 'Where is the car, *bibi*?' he asked, worried.

Pat came the reply: 'In the river.'

Contributed by Shalini Dayal, Nagpur

ODE TO GHALIB

For the sigh to be effective it needed an age,
    So, for the most part obscure you stayed,
Now, with the fool and the wise alike, as
    you have become a rage
And in your name now as fortunes are being made,
    On this turning of the wheel
Tell me, *Mirza*, how exactly you feel.

    Do you still smart under the infamy,
humiliation and hurt?

    From your creditors are you hiding still?
What do you have to say
    About the cliques and the patronage,
Of your day and our age?

    About your poetry's greatness
When there is universal 'yes',
    I will only add my humble acclaim
And kiss your verses and your name.

    But with these matters I'll some other time
    deal
For now, tell me pray: How do you feel?

Contributed by Kuldip Salil, Delhi

FREE GIFT

 Banta Singh rushed back angrily to the grocery shop from where he had purchased a packet of butter few minutes ago.

'Where is my free gift?' he shouted at the shopkeeper. 'But sir, there is no free gift on the purchase of butter,' the shopkeeper answered politely.

'Don't fool me,' replied Banta, 'It is clearly written on the packet of the butter: "Cholesterol free".'

Contributed by Rakhi Guleria, Nasik

PURIST AT WORK

What will Santa do after taking photocopies?

He will compare them with the original for spelling mistakes!

Contributed by Sweta Nadkarni, Noida

SWEETLY TIMED

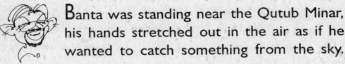Banta was standing near the Qutub Minar, his hands stretched out in the air as if he wanted to catch something from the sky.

A passerby saw him and asked what he was doing.

Banta replied, 'When I was upstairs my watch fell off, so I came down to catch it!'

'But if your watch fell down so long ago, how can you catch it now?'

'My dear,' assured Banta, 'my watch is always half an hour late!'

Contributed by Ruchi Singh, Mumbai

ANSWERING MACHINE BLUES

Santa bought a new answering machine for his home in Punjab but disconnected it within two days. When his friends asked him the reason for disconnecting the new answering machine, Santa said, 'I am getting a bad response. My friends say things like, "*Saala....phone utha ke kehta hai ki, 'main ghar pe nahin hoon'!*"' (Stupid... picks up the phone and says he is not home!)

Contributed by Abigyan Hans, Bangalore

A FAIRER IMAGE

Three *sardarjis* went to fish. One of them caught a mermaid. The mermaid begged them to let her go. Each of them wanted a boon. She agreed to it.

The first *sardarji* asked to double his IQ. So the mermaid granted his wish.

The second *sardarji* asked to triple his IQ. His wish was granted too.

And the third *sardarji* asked to quintuple his IQ.

The mermaid warned him about the consequences; that his image might be changed.

But he insisted. At once the mermaid granted his wish and he became a *sardarani*!

Contributed by Shubhadeep Guha, Siliguri

WITH A MESSAGE

Why does Santa have 'TGIF' written on his shoes?

Toes Go In First.

Contributed by Dinesh Prabhu, Pune

HIS FATHER'S SON

Santa fell in love and wanted to marry Kunwarjeet. He was excited at the prospect of marriage and told his father Banta Singh, of his intentions.

'Dear Santa' said his father, 'you'll have to find another girl. Your mother doesn't know, but Kunwarjeet is your half-sister.'

So Santa dutifully forgot about his Kunwarjeet and fell in love with Kiran. He approached his father again and told him about Kiran.

His father objected again, 'You can't marry Kiran, my boy, and please don't tell your mother, because Kunwar and Kiran and several more I know are your half-sisters.'

When Santa's mother learnt about this she said, 'Dear Santa, do what makes you happy. Marry Kunwar or marry Kiran, because Banta is not your father!'

Contributed by Rakhi Rai, Kolkata

OMBAY ! OMBAY !

SOUND OF SILENCE

Once Indira Gandhi and Zail Singh were travelling in the same car to Bombay.

Zail Singh was going to Bombay for the first time. He was naturally very excited and could not hold on to his excitement and started singing, 'Bombay, Bombay...Bombay.'

This excitement of Zail Singh upset Indira and she said, 'Be silent!'

On hearing that Zail Singh started singing, 'Ombay, ombay....ombay!'

Contributed by Karanjit Kaur, Kanpur

CRICKET IN HEAVEN

Santa and Banta were great cricket fanatics. They decided that whoever died first would try to come back in the other's dreams, and would talk about cricket in Heaven.

Santa died first. One day, when he was fast asleep, Banta heard Santa calling him to talk about cricket. Banta was happy and eager to know about cricket in Heaven.

'So, Santa! How is cricket in Heaven?

Replied Santa, 'Hey, Banta, I have good news and bad news. The good news is that tomorrow we are going to have a day and night match here in Heaven. And the bad news is that you are the opening bowler for tomorrow's match!'

Contributed by Farzan Ahmed, Pune

NOISY SUICIDE

 Santa Singh hurried into the emergency room late one night, with the tip of his index finger shot off.

'How did this happen?' the emergency room doctor asked him.

'Well, I was trying to commit suicide,' Santa replied.

'What?' sputtered the doctor. 'You tried to commit suicide by shooting your finger off?'

'No! No! No! I put the gun to my ear, and I thought: "This is going to make a loud noise." So I put my finger in the other ear before I pulled the trigger.'

Contributed by P.S. Sethi, Patiala

ANOTHER EXAMPLE!

 In a medical college practical exam, during viva, the doctor asked Santa: 'Can you give an example of an amphibian?'

Santa Singh replied: 'A frog.'

Doctor: 'Very good. Can you give another example?' asked the doctor.

'Another frog!' answered Santa Singh.

Contributed by Siddhartha Kumar, Shimla

WITH APOLOGIES TO *GURUDEV*

Years after Independence,
    an ordinary Indian bewails:
Where peoples' reps don't dare
move without Zed security,
    Where school doors are slammed on the
    kids without capitation fee,
Where the society is broken up into minorities,
    Sawarnas, SCs and OBCs,
Where daily new words like Bofors, *Chara* and
    Hawala get currency,
Where hands need grease to reach the nearest
file.
    Where *kattas*, guns and bombs are the latest
    reasoning style,
Where thought and action are confined to narrow,
    still narrower identity,
Into that abyss of gloom and despair,
    Why, oh why, my father, was the country
    led by thee?

Contributed by A.P. Kishra, Allahabad

'BREAKING NEWS'

Stolen Painting Found by Tree.

•

Two Soviet Ships Collide, One Dies.

•

Killer Sentenced to Die for Second Time in 10 Years.

•

War Dims Hope for Peace.

•

If Strike isn't Settled Quickly, It May Last a While.

•

Cold Wave Linked to Temperatures.

•

Couple Slain; Police Suspect Homicide.

•

Red Tape Holds Up New Bridge.

•

Man Struck by Lightning Faces Battery Charge.

•

New Study of Obesity Looks for Larger Test Group.

•

Astronaut Takes Blame for Gas in Spacecraft.

HOT & COLD

Santa was looking at a thermos in a store when the sales girl walked upto him and asked, 'May I help you with anything, sir?'

'Yes! What is that?'

'Why, that's a thermos!'

'What does it do?'

'It keeps things hot and it keeps things cold!'

'I'll take it,' said Santa.

The next day Santa went to work carrying this thermos. His co-workers asked him what he was carrying.

'It's a thermos.'

'What does it do?'

'It keeps things hot and it keeps things cold!'

'So what have you got in it?'

'An icecream and a cup of coffee.'

Contributed by Sanjoy Mitra, Asansol

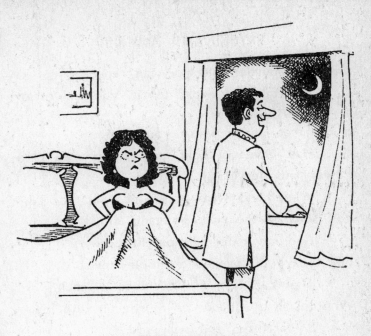

MOONY MADNESS

For their honeymoon, they hired a room in a hotel. Night had fallen and the bride had dressed herself in a provocative negligee, and was in bed. The bridegroom was fully dressed and was gazing out of the window at the moon. After an hour the bride asked him, 'Why don't you come to bed?'

He replied, 'Never mind me, you go to sleep. My mother told me that this would be the most wonderful night that I would see, and I don't want to miss a minute of it.'

Contributed by Lt. Col. (Retd.) P. B. Sarpeshkar, Bangalore

BEYOND MAN AND GOD

You can murder and you can rape,
        And take my word for it, you will escape
        scotfree
If the tree under which you stand
        Has leaves of gold, and is manured with
Power and perversity.
        Wheel and steal or kill at will,
You sons of the rich, go gaily amuck
        And never for a moment bother,
For I have discovered a simple device
        That can turn a BMW into a truck.
Whether it is *Tandoor* or murder in the Inn,
        I guarantee, you will win.
Fear not, dear, for the law is one of your inlaws,
        And those who enforce it know too well
        your worth,
Fear no power divine or terrestrial,
        For great God is asleep in heaven
And all is well with the earth.

Contributed by Kuldip Salil, Delhi